THE 5 UNDERGROUND SECRETS USED BY THE TOP 1% OF ONLINE MARKETERS

THE 5 UNDERGROUND SECRETS USED BY THE TOP 1% OF ONLINE MARKETERS

DISCOVER HOW THE TOP 1% GROW HUNGRY AUDIENCES IN 30 DAYS OR LESS

Kendra Fipps Crowe

ISBN: 979-8-218-19921-0

Published by:
Achieving Higher Results LCC
5343 Belleville Crossing Street #2099
Belleville, IL 62226
kendracrowe.com/hi

Cover Photo by GSB Mohib Khan
Interior Formatting and Design by KingdomCovers.com

Disclaimer: The author makes no guarantees concerning the level of success you may experience by following the advice and strategies contained in this book, and you accept the risk that results will differ for each individual. The testimonials and examples provided in this book show exceptional results, which may not apply to the average reader, and are not intended to represent or guarantee that you will achieve the same or similar results.

Contents

Foreword by Cedrick Harris

"All I can say is WOW . . .

It's been 14 years since I first met Kendra Fipps Crowe. During that time I have had the delight of watching her grow tremendously as a marketer and influencer. Thru masterminds, traveling around the world, zooms, 3-plus hour phone calls, long drives together, and more, her intelligence in the marketplace has increased 10 fold.

After reading this book, I know for sure everyone who really absorbs what she is saying will see tremendous success in their business. Every chapter is laid out perfectly walking you thru the exact steps needed to thrive in the current business world. The amount of market research, time, study, and more importantly, tested facts, is second to none.

Reading a business book can be boring at times. However, Kendra has laid this out in a very exciting way so you can absorb these tactics and be able to implement them with ease. After being in the marketing game for over 24 years, I have picked up some golden nuggets myself that I have implemented with tremendous results. Don't take the words lightly . . . Don't skim thru the chapters, there's actually gold in this book and once you apply these techniques, your bank account will thank you for it!

As a friend of Kendra's, I'm so happy this book is published and will be able to help so many people. The million-dollar question is simple . . . WILL YOU BE ONE OF THEM?"

Cedrick Harris
CEO & Founder of Team Takeover Marketing

Foreword by Dr. Marquel Russell

I have Good news and Bad News . . .

Let's start with the Good News . . .

The "e-learning" aka "online marketing" industry is one of the fastest growing industries in the world with no signs of slowing down (expected value of $645 billion by 2030)!

Now for the Bad News . . .

While the online marketing industry is like the modern day gold rush, most people have no clue that it exists and many of those that know that it exist, have no clue how to get their piece of this MASSIVE pie!

The BETTER News is that Kendra has graciously put this masterpiece of a book together for you to get the strategies to build your own empire using the internet and create a fortune for you and your family, like many of us have done.

Actually, calling this a book is disrespectful.

Consider this a key to the vault that unlocks riches that most keep to themselves.

I've personally watched Kendra quietly help build empires online over the years.

She's architected multi-million dollar businesses and has been the secret weapon for one of my earlier mentors who'd you'd definitely know if name dropping was my thing, and she's worked with some of the brightest minds of the last century.

What I will say is this . . .

If you let this book sit on your desk or bookshelf or your hard drive and just collect physical or digital dust like most people do, just know that you're literally letting an uncashed, blank check just sit there and it has an expiration date.

Do yourself a favor . . . don't wait.

Continue reading, get out your highlighter and your notebook and start implementing the game plan Kendra has mapped out for you to build a business that affords you the time and financial freedom that you desire and deserve.

I looked forward to hearing your success story!

Dr. Marquel Russell
The King Of Client Attraction
CEO & Co-Founder of Client Attraction University

Foreword by Jerome Lewis

It is my honor to write a foreword for *The 5 Underground Secrets Used by the Top 1% of Online Marketers*. This book is written by Kendra, a highly skilled marketer and a wonderful person with a sincere desire to help others succeed. I have had the privilege of working with Kendra for several years, and I can attest to her exceptional marketing skills and her unwavering commitment to helping others reach their goals.

Kendra has worked with some of the most successful professionals and millionaires in the world of online marketing, and she has honed her skills through years of hard work and dedication. In this book, she shares the secrets that have helped her to become one of the top 1% of online marketers, and she does so in a way that is both insightful and actionable. Whether you are a seasoned marketer or just starting out, this book will provide you with the knowledge and strategies you need to succeed in the competitive world of online marketing.

Throughout the book, Kendra provides a wealth of information on the latest trends and techniques in online marketing. And she does so in a way that is easy to understand and apply. Whether you are looking to improve your SEO, drive more traffic to your website, or increase conversions, Kendra's expertise and guidance will help you achieve your goals.

In addition to her marketing skills, Kendra's passion and commitment to helping others succeed are truly inspiring. Her love for marketing is evident in every word she writes, and her genuine desire to help others is evident in every page of this book. Whether you are a seasoned marketer or just starting out, this book will provide you with the knowledge and insights you need to succeed in the world of online marketing.

In conclusion, I highly recommend *The 5 Underground Secrets Used by the Top 1% of Online Marketers* to anyone looking to succeed in the world of online marketing. Kendra's expertise and passion are evident on every page, and her commitment to helping others succeed is truly inspiring. Whether you are a seasoned marketer or just starting out, this book will provide you with the knowledge and strategies you need to succeed.

Jerome Lewis
Marketing Implementation Expert

The Most Incredible FREE Gift Ever!

$997.94 Worth of Pure
Money-Making Information

Kendra Fipps Crowe offers an incredible opportunity
for you to see why the Kendra Crowe Inner Circle
is known as the place for growth where entrepreneurs seeking fast and dramatic growth and greater
control, independence, and security come together.
Kendra wants to give you $997.94 worth of pure
money-making information, including a free masterclass. You will receive a free all-access pass to this
private masterclass where she will give you every marketing advantage to grow your business. Sign up for
free. Go to: https://titans3000.com

I know without her, I would have been
stuck several times. She gets business and
entrepreneurship, especially making money online.

—Jim Beard, Riverview, Michigan

Dedication

To my son, Adrian: This book is dedicated to you. Our family suffered a huge loss when you made your transition to be with the Lord. My job as your advocate for more than twenty-nine years is over. Thank you for allowing me to be your mom.

To my family: I so appreciate your support. Thank you for believing in me.

To my mom, Bobbie Jean: Thank you for your constant willingness to give a listening ear to my marketing adventures. I'm so grateful for a mom like you.

To my second mom, Bobbie Jean #2: More than fifteen years ago, you took me on as your daughter and I never looked back. The Lord knew I need two Bobbie Jeans, and I'm so honored He gave you both to me.

Connect with Kendra

https://www.facebook.com/kendralfipps/

https://www.instagram.com/kendrafippscrowe/

https://www.linkedin.com/in/kendrafipps/

Dear Friend,

I WILL UNVEIL A secret in this book: how the top 1% grow their business. The goal of this book is to get you to play the game of the top 1%.

Why?

You are inundated with so many marketing messages (according to Forbes.com, it's up to 10,000 a day[1]), you are bound to feel overwhelmed and even misled. How can you find someone you can trust?

The top 1% wants to remain at the top, so they hide information from you, thus making the entire process of growing a business hard for you to understand. They

[1] https://www.forbes.com/sites/johnhall/2019/08/25/how-to-get-your-marketing-to-cut-through-the-noise/?sh=6f04750d3a84 accessed January 19, 2023

do not do magic or perform miracles; they simply follow a rule and process religiously until it works for them. So don't waste your hard-earned money, which I know is important to you. The challenge of making a wise decision about who to go to for help is all too common and more important than ever.

My name is Kendra Fipps Crowe, and I make the entire process of getting more customers simple and easy for you to understand. I have been in this field for many years, and all you need to do is to follow the steps I have outlined in this book.

I want to remove any fears, frustration, or confusion as you go through this process. That's why I created this book: *The Underground Secrets Used by the Top 1% to Get More Customers.*

In the pages that follow, you will discover exactly which questions to ask so that you can make an informed decision about choosing the right program for effective customer acquisition.

It's been designed in a simple, easy-to-understand way so that new customers come to you and you can sleep at night, knowing rent and payroll are covered—which is what you want and deserve.

Okay, let's get started!

Why Should You Listen to Me?

I AM A BUSINESS COACH, MENTOR, and mother of two kids, one with special needs. My son was diagnosed at an early age with a form of meningitis. With that level of care, I had to find a way to provide for my family and be present for my children. My biggest struggle was to find a balance between doctor visits, ER visits, school outings, and meetings. What mattered most to me was the ability to have freedom to schedule my time. At the time of writing of this book, my son has made his transition to be with the Lord. We are so blessed to have had him with us for over twenty-nine years. He left irreplaceable memories in our lives.

My four siblings and I were raised by a single mom, which made finances were super tight. While we were growing up, our little family was poor. We didn't have money for school clothes, and I had to chop and pick cotton for the necessities. So I don't mind hard work. Our mom installed in us to take responsibility for ourselves at an early age. It's not what happens to you; it's what you do with what happens to you.

I started my first company in an office with two friends. The goal was just to market T-shirts. Little did I know, I would get a phone call from a seven-figure income earner to become his assistant. I dropped my friends, or I should say, they dropped me. And the rest was history.

With several failed businesses, I never wanted to give up. Now I can smell a failing business a mile away. I knew the next opportunity would be better; all I had to do was work harder. And of course, that wasn't true.

From my first brush with success, we had a system. We create a list of prospects, which led to leads and then to customers. I lost that aha moment for years. One day, my boss said we were going to an event. And all my past experience came back to me. When you create a list of buyers, you can take them with you, no matter where you go.

My success with creating systems, using tools, growing audiences, and event planning gave way to an opportunity to become a marketing director for an international company. In this position, I saw firsthand what business owners were looking for in a marketing company for new customers. This was a very long and drawn-out process.

My heart dropped to see how this company had so many hands in the process but nothing could get done. And amazingly, the top 1% in this domain had many more customers than they were able to serve. Most of them outsource customers to others to deliver in the specified timeframe. So I made a commitment moving forward to over deliver and get fast results for my customers.

If you're like my average client, currently struggling to get new customers using a broken system, the buck stops here. If you are done with hiring marketing companies or gurus that don't care about you, buying ads that seem beyond your budget, and feeling as if you can't trust anyone to guide you through this, I am here to help.

This book has been carefully written to take you from your current position to being among the top 1%. This is because your position is very critical for the success of any agency or organization. From personal experience, I have watched a company lose twenty-five thousand dollars with an ad agency without a single sale. It was not an easy process to watch because I wasn't in control of that marketing plan. But now, you will have the tools to make better decisions than they did. I have seen both sides of the coin. For over a decade, I have been working alongside a seven-figure income earner, and I will share how they move and think in this book.

Okay, now that you know a little about me, let's get into what you need to know to get more new customers so you can sleep tonight.

THE 5 UNDERGROUND SECRETS USED BY THE Top 1% OF ONLINE MARKETERS

How to Attract Your Dream Clients?

WHAT IF EVERYTHING you've been told about getting more customers was completely false? Throughout the next few pages, you will discover how a massive movement of business owners increased their bottom line and gained new customers all by using the skills and services of the top 1%.

When I first understood how important the first secret was, I was blown away. One of my mentors shared a story with me about how a major Fortune 500 company made all of their decisions about how to market their products and who they marketed to. It was centered on their customer avatar.

Imagine sitting with the owners and the chief marketing office in the boardroom on the 15 floor around a large cherry and oak table with coffee being served by an assistant. The discussion opens with what does their customer want? What conversations are they currently having? What problems is Billy facing this week? How can we help Mary and Don solve their son Billy's biggest problem: increasing his confidence to go to prom? The boardroom walls had photo for each of customer. This company sold skin care products to parents with kids struggling with self-esteem problems.

The customers had names, photos, and what problems they were facing with their son. The company even knew that Billy was going to prom. I asked, "Wait. Is this true?" And my mentor said, "Yes, this happens every day." This top 1% has learned to get into the conversation being had by their customers in their minds and homes.

Do you have names or photos for your clients or customers? Do you know the problems they are facing currently? Do you know what conversations are being had about their problems or challenges? How much do you really know about your clients or customers? If you are still convinced that your product is for everyone, shame on you. Stop taking money out of your children's education fund because you are unwilling to do market research. It's time for you to roll up your shelves and do the work. And even if you get this half right, you may see an increase in your profits. As you continue to read on, you will see the guide I've given you to help you get started with your first customer avatar profile.

The truth of the matter is this: When you speak to everyone, you speak to no one. Most coaches and consultants feel that everyone needs their services. That is far from the truth. In your current business, you may have customers who you don't like. You may feel that you are attracting the wrong type of customers or that you just need the right customers to keep the doors open.

How? Discover the Power of a Client Avatar

Imagine if your ideal clients were always coming your way. Imagine if you fired those clients that regularly requested chargebacks or refunds, the complainers, the blamers, and the negative reviewers. How does that sound? Great, right? The top 1% doesn't want you to know how they became the top 1% and how they stay there. This secret is the client avatar. A client avatar is the profiling of your clients with their name, demographics, goals, values, challenges, etc. An ideal client avatar defines, models, or simulates an individual who represents the average characteristics of your target audience. If you can develop a specific client avatar, then you will get closer to play in the league of the top 1%. The top 1% knows how to get into the conversation their clients are having and leverage this to into massive sales.

As you prepare to play at a higher level, the first goal is to let go of the nightmare clients so you can focus on your ideal clients. This way, you are left with only those loyal clients, your true fan base, clients who are ready to buy your product, regardless of the price. They know your true worth, so you can charge more. For me, this is the first thing I do for any product I manage, and truly, it has been a positive turning point that has yielded much profit for every one.

Creating the Ideal Client Avatar

Creating an ideal client avatar requires you to know your client at a deeper level. You need to connect with them to truly understand their needs and requirements. Connecting with your clients spans beyond knowing their names and, if possible, emotionally connecting with them. The three Cs of a client avatar include:

- connect

- capture

- convert

However, you cannot generalize or play at the bottom of the game; the top 1% do more and take great care to distinguish themselves in this market or industry. They employ a lot of business management theories and skills to retain people. Let us take a look at the three Cs:

- Connect: This is not only normal connection but goes beyond networking into a combination of the two. Take a look at relationships. For example, two strangers meet up and begin to share stories about themselves, their pasts, experiences, and family backgrounds. Within a short time, they connect as though they have known each other for years. This is how to create true connections. When you are creating a client avatar, try to add items that will help you connect, such as what they like, hate, or their previous experiences. Learn their name, address, preferences, etc. Create a short video to talk directly to them; this way, they learn about you and convert to a sale.

- Capture: The goal of creating a connection is to eventually capture your ideal clients. The capture process will require you to deepen your connection and capture your client's interest.

- Convert: Once you've captured your connection, you want to convert them to loyal clients. Without creating this avatar or without a deeper understanding of your clients, your message will sound like all the other messages out there.

The top 1% hide this secret from you, but big companies employ this strategy. Your ideal client avatar can be revised as often as you want, but first, you have to start. Don't procrastinate. The best time to start is now. I will show you how to create one.

The Ideal Client Avatar

An avatar is simply creating characteristics or features of your best clients. Creating an avatar is more like writing a story of your clients and describing their lives and experiences that will lead them to your product. Imagine what is important to them: their goals and challenges. When you know the story of their life, when you are creating an avatar video, you can speak directly to them. Remember, as a potential top 1% earner, your goal is not to reach everyone but to focus on your loyal fans. Thus, you want to speak to them as though you are going through the same challenges they are facing. Talk about wearing the same shoes, sharing the same goals, and having the same values.

You need to carefully develop a client avatar. Don't rush this process because it will determine the rest of your journey. The following metrics will help you know your clients and create an avatar. Remember, you can have two avatars, and businesses commonly do that.

- Gender: Are your clients male or female or evenly mixed?

- Age: How old are they? What is the age bracket?

- Income range: Are they low-, average-, or high-income earners?

- Occupation: What do they do? Are you targeting any specific occupations?

- Marital status: Are they married? Single? Divorced? Do they have children?

- Location: Where do they live? Are they city, suburban, or rural dwellers?

Now, these metrics help you narrow down to a specific target group and understand their characteristics, possible struggles, challenges, goals, desires, etc. When you create an avatar, you have taken a step to distinguish yourself. You can find their likes on Facebook or other social media platforms. You can learn where they love to shop, what their favorite movies or books are, etc. The more you know, the more beneficial to you your avatar becomes.

Use the following form to create your ideal client avatar.

Avatar Name (Company or Individual Name)

CEO Name:

Age:

Gender:

Marital status:

Number of children:

Age of children:

Location:

Quote:

Occupation:

How to Attract Your Dream Clients?

Job title:

Annual income:

Level of education:

Other:

Goals and Values

Goals:

Values:

Challenges and Pain Points

Challenges:

Pain points:

Sources of Information

Books:

Magazines:

Conferences:

Blogs/website:

Gurus:

Others:

Objections and Roles in Purchase Process

Objections to the sale:

Role in purchase process:

SECRET #2: STOP THE
MARKETING ROLLERCOASTER
- RAPID TRUST AND
WELCOME PACKAGES

What is a Shock and Awe Package?

ONE OF THE key components of marketing is creating a bond with your target audience. With relationships, building customer loyalty and retention is a breeze. The idea is to make customers trust and relate to your brand by first prioritizing them.

Marketing shouldn't end with telling them about your business and what they stand to gain by patronizing you. Go the extra mile by letting gifts do the talking. These are a powerful yet simple way to catch their attention and pave the way for a potentially successful relationship.

Even better, this works for both new and existing customers. It sends the message that you are thinking of them, which many will find warm and charming. You'd be surprised at how you can make people smile with small, thoughtful gifts.

Types of Packages

The Rapid Trust and Welcome Packages

This one secret gets me so excited because I'm a huge giver. When you build your business off of giving, you will always get a return. When you give someone a gift, it is a natural response to do something in return. But more about that later. Let me share how I have been personally affected by this secret.

When I first joined a company about 17 years ago as an affiliate with the company. I was excited about the opportunity. One day, I went to the mailbox and found a card welcoming me to the team. It had a beautiful photo of my mentor and his team. Still, to this day, I'm associated with this company.

What mattered to me most was his thoughtfulness over the years.

People will forget what you said to them, but they will never forget how you made them feel. I know this secret will have some of you rolling your eyes, but for those who find ways to implement this secret into your business, you will reap the rewards. So get outside of your comfort zone and try it. What's the worst thing that could happen: You gain more returning customers? Most top 1% have built their business on this secret alone.

The Prospecting Package:

The prospecting stage is when you first reach out to customers on a personal level. It's a crucial part of the marketing build-up and plays a key role in whether you can develop a relationship with them now and in the future. Unfortunately, however, many marketers find this stage challenging or even impossible.

If you find yourself in a bind, trying to get through to customers, why not try a gift? A prospecting gift opens the door for a conversation. Think of it as a middle ground, where customers are more than happy to hear you out, a welcome package that speaks for you and your brand. For the best results, consider personalized gifts tailored to each prospect. The sales process is more likely to go in your favor afterward.

The more intentional you are about prospective gifts, the better your chances are for a solid, lasting relationship. As a matter of fact, most marketers confirm that personalization takes customer relationships to new heights. Every prospect is different, after all. It makes sense to treat them as such.

The Check-In Package:

This is the "just because" package with no underlying motive. It's a way to market yourself without trying to convince the customer of anything. There's no special occasion. You aren't trying to convince them to buy anything yet. But it remains a powerful medium of communication.

It shows the customers that they are always in your thoughts, and you don't need a special reason to appreciate them. This sort of gesture draws them to you, and they start to think of you in a different light.

For this package, you want to give them something handy, like a coffee mug or a kitchen napkin. It should be something that they will put to daily use, thus serving as a reminder to them and as an ad to visitors.

Why Should You Care?

The Reciprocal Altruism Rule:

At the top of this rule is the belief that we give gifts to get gifts in return. In marketing, it means gifting prospective customers to drive business. The concept is relatively simple; you would think more marketers would leverage it. For instance, suppose you have a friend that fixes gadgets: phones, laptops, computers, the whole nine yards. One day, your laptop won't turn on, so you give them a call. They drop everything to come and take a look and get it going again. You try to pay them, but they wave you off. In the future, if someone close to you were in a similar situation, you would probably refer that friend to them.

Why's that? When someone goes out of their way to give you a gift or do you a favor, your perception of them changes. Humans are naturally inclined to feel indebted when someone offers us things with no strings attached. As such, we are wired to repay their generosity, often with something similar or better. So you would be inclined to take your gadgets to them again and refer others too.

Improve Brand Recall:

The drip campaign in marketing is all about staying in touch with your customers. And as far as actions go, gifting speaks louder than words. Sending your customers thoughtful gifts is the fastest way to place your brand at the forefront of their minds. That means better recall and more word-of-mouth advertisements. This also means that one customer could single-handedly lift your brand visibility and reach. It's a gold mine.

Customer Engagement:

A simple "remember me" or "thank you" gift to customers is a great way to convert leads and encourage repeat business. The same goes for incentives that reward customers for referring your brand to others. All of these culminate in customer engagement.

It's normal for existing customers to forget about you over time for various reasons. But a simple gift can help reinstate your brand in their lives. It conveys that their continued patronage is an essential part of the success and growth of your business in the long run.

In addition, the more personalized and thoughtful the gift is, the more goodwill you spread, which can trigger a barrage of positive reviews and feelings. It shows that you care about client satisfaction and are interested in their welfare. And since we live in interesting times, when people share their lives on social media, you could potentially be looking at new leads and quality referrals.

Who Should Handle the Package?

There is a business for just about everything these days. So it's easy to outsource gifting, leaving someone else to do all the brain work while you focus on other things. I highly recommend https://amcards.com for your needs. Curtis Lewsey is a great friend, and his company has invested a lot in appreciation marketing. While this helps free up time and saves you what could potentially be backbreaking work, outsourcing gifting might lack that personal touch needed to connect with your audience.

You want others to feel as if you thought of them and genuinely wanted to reach out. Customers want to feel as if there is more to the business than their frequent purchase—that you see them for who they are: Humans just trying their best. This takes us to the next point.

What Should You Give?

It might help to steer clear of generic gifts, such as tumblers, stickers, key holders, and the like. Many other businesses will give out those. The last thing you want is to drown clients in generic gifts.

Set yourself apart with something that holds their attention, such as a book you wrote or a free report. A welcome card can also be a fine way to break the ice with new clients. They have to read it to learn about your message. You have their attention at that moment, and your message might be the final tug needed to reel them in and give you the edge over competitors.

Is This Marketing Trick Any Good?

A large percentage of customers don't want to have a relationship with a brand. For them, the relationship is strictly business, and interactions ought to be limited to invitations to sales or discounts. For these types of customers, relationships are reserved for loved ones, not businesses.

However, some customers don't agree with this sentiment. A small percentage, yes, but they believe they could and should have relationships with the businesses they buy from.

Now, you have two contrasting customers. It shouldn't be difficult trying to cater to both sides. Don't attempt to become cuddly with customers who don't want a relationship by reaching out regularly through frequent emails, text messages, and checking-in gifts. If anything, you will only drive them further away. Save that for customers who are keen on building a relationship. The top 1% understand how to segment their list through multiple campaigns.

This is important for you to know because most businesses struggle to pull in a consistent flow of new customers. You have great weeks and then days with no customers. Your unpredictable income has serious consequences on your mental health and as to if you will be able to keep the doors open. Some you of get so frustrated in the process of searching for the right fit, you begin to believe there is no hope for you. And some of you believe that marketing is best outsourced.

One of my faithful customers reached out to me, asking if I could please help her with marketing. She said, "I enjoy getting referrals, but some weeks, my business slows way down. I know my business needs a way to get new customers in addition to keeping my happy customers. I'm on several social media platforms, and I feel like it is a waste of time. Can you help me?"

Here's what you need to do to get off the marketing roller coaster. Success leaves clues. Disney World has the best marketing plan to convert new customers I have ever seen. Let's take a closer into their business. They have procedures or a step-by-step plan for everything they offer. You can do the same with acquiring new customers.

Creating the right plan for you starts with asking these simple questions. Who are the best customers for me?

Does my message resonate with them? Last but not least, am I getting the best return on my marketing investment (ROI)? Most entrepreneurs don't hold their marketing dollars accountable. Don't let that be you. "What do you mean by that, Kendra?" For every dollar you spend, you will get a dollar out plus.

SECRET #3: CAN I DO
THIS MYSELF?

How to Build an Audience From Nothing

WHILE THE TOP 1% is highly engaged in every step of their marketing plan, as well as likely employing an agency, you absolutely can do this for yourself. Most business owners focus on serving clients and outsource the marketing to an agency. I urge you to be very active in the process. You are not in the coaching, consulting, or chiropractic business; you are in the marketing business.

You might offer great products or services, but without an audience, you have no business. The market is there all right. You just have to convince them to look your way.

Many businesses struggle to capture their target market's attention, especially small businesses. One could argue that business is all about fighting for the market's attention, and that would be correct.

The problem isn't that the market isn't interested. It's that consumers, how people learn, and even the economy have changed. Buyers don't learn about and purchase products and services using the old and conventional channels. So you have to learn about the new solutions that they prefer. These are sophisticated because these buyers are more inclined to solve their own problems. That's why there is such an outburst of communities, social media, and word-of-mouth advertisements. Customers find what they need through these mediums.

Studies prove the influence of social media on purchasing decisions and how people shop for their needs[1]. As a result, your marketing has to make the jump so that you can deal with the new system. The use of traditional mediums—conferences, trade magazine ads, and trade-show booths—are now recipes for disaster. If you must break through to this new age of buyers, you first have

---

1   Timothy, Dotsey. (2019). The influence of social media on consumer buying behavior: a case study of Ho Technical University, Ho.

to collect valuable information, process it into content, and deliver value to the market.

In this section, we will explore how to create market demand for your products or services, capture the attention of your preferred customer type, and funnel them toward your business through social media as a tool. The top 1% create massive audiences to build their list; they believe that money is in the size of their list. The bigger the list, the more money they will earn. We currently coach our clients to maximize social media.

Here are five steps to use:

Study the market:

The top 1% discover their market and know the ins and outs of their industry. The first step to capturing the market is unraveling the identity of your target audience. It doesn't matter how large your audience is; some common ground will unite them. And you don't want to limit yourself to generic demographics, e.g., seniors earning thirty to fifty thousand per year through pensions and investments. Dive deep beyond the surface. Learn what incentivizes them to search for solutions—pain points that they seek to resolve.

Learning about what motivates them is crucial and makes for a more complete and effective sales pipeline.

Many marketers rely on their gut feelings, thinking they know their audiences well enough. But if history has shown us anything, it's that data trumps guts most of the time.

Create and establish a social media presence:

It goes without saying that a social media presence is now imperative for businesses. You do not need one because every one else does, but you do need one as an avenue to invest a significant amount of your marketing budget and strategies.

Why? Well, for one, over 4.48 billion people use social media[2]. That's almost half of the global population. It's easily one of the largest markets in the world, just waiting to be harnessed. Even better, it doesn't cost a thing to create and own an account.

With a viable marketing strategy, social media is a handy tool for penetrating and carving out a place for yourself in the market. But without a solid strategy, you will waste valuable resources, and your efforts to pursue any goals will be futile.

A solid strategy entails establishing a presence and a reputation for pushing the right content at the right time to the right audience.

2   https://backlinko.com/social-media-users Accessed January 19, 2023

Create valuable content:

Once you set up a social media account, the next step is crucial to your brand image and how the market perceives and responds to you. On social media, content is king. You want to focus on two types of content: internal and external.

Internal content is the posts you create for your brand while external content is acquired from quality sources. Internal content is proof that you know your worth and the best industry practices. External content proves that you can spot trends and serve your audience. Most successful brands combine both forms of content for balance and scalability.

You can convey external content to your audiences through several methods: new insightful research into current industry trends, webinars, virtual or in-person conferences, the latest and vital news from your line of business and other relevant subjects, in-depth white papers, e-books and guides, infographics, social calendars with relevant dates and resources, etc.

Create a like-campaign ad:

The more likes your social media accounts generate, the higher your social proof. Customers tend to judge authenticity by page engagements. And while this isn't always a true depiction of authenticity, there's an argument to be made for such sentiments.

Page like ad campaigns are paid adverts designed to improve the amount of visibility your social media account or page receive, thereby increasing your likes. The advertisement targets people who are inclined to buy your products, services, or brand in general, and those who might be interested in your content. If this person is intrigued by your ads, they are more likely to answer your call to action (CTA) and interact with your brand. Recall that we shared earlier how important it is to create your customer avatar. Now take this information and insert it in your campaign.

Setting up a page like ad campaigns isn't difficult. Depending on the social media network, you can find it in the ads manager section. Alternatively, you could use ad solutions, e.g., AdEspresso.

Create a new campaign and fill out the objective. On AdEspresso, you will find an option for Page Likes. Select to continue to finalize the ad campaign.

Grow and manage engagement:

Engagement refers to how people deal with your brand and the content you create. It could mean their reactions, shares, likes, comments, and even views. While all these forms of engagement are great in their own rights, shares are the best deal of the lot.

You can't get engagement without quality content, so you have to entertain leads to move clients further down the sales pipeline. Think infographics, blog posts, case studies, reviews, tutorials, and other content that your customers find useful. The idea is to use regular value content to promote your brand and boost engagement to improve market reach.

At this point, you should already have your content on lock, knowing what type to use and what customers expect.

So begin creating internal content, sharing external content, and testing engagement to discover the format and style that is best received by your audience.

Finally, commit to delivering regular content. You start to lose customers if you struggle to deliver content frequently. As a rule of thumb, this is four to eight times each day. Don't be vanilla either. Mix things up. Use live videos, infographics, polls, videos, pictures, etc.

Creating a huge audience is paramount for your business. You must leverage what you have. I call it a blessing and a curse at the same time. Most business owners don't know what to do, where to start, or how to get their audience to raise their hands and ask for more. People buy from those they like, know, and trust.

I worked with a fitness trainer who didn't have an audience on Facebook. He struggled to get in front of the right customers. So I helped him find a niche where he created an audience of more than twenty thousand fans who wanted to get fit.

Currently, you may be using social media platforms (Facebook, Instagram, or Twitter) to promote, increase brand awareness, or invite customers to your offer. Let's face it, Facebook has become a daily part of our customers' lives.

Facebook is the leading social platform with 59 percent of social media users.[3] There are more than 200 million small business around the world using Facebook Tools.[4] And last but not least, 63.7 percent of the US population over the age of thirteen use Facebook, according to DataReportal.[5] If you shy away from using Facebook, at least you know where your customers might be. However, some have lost their shirt trying to use the platform.

You must use all forms of media to reach your ideal client. I will share how to dramatically increase your audience, which will lead to new customers. With a few simple tweaks, new customers will want what you have.

3   https://backlinko.com/social-media-users Accessed January 19, 2023

4   https://www.businessdit.com/business-on-facebook-statistics/. Accessed January 19, 2023

5   https://datareportal.com/reports/digital-2022-united-states-of-america. Accessed January 19, 2023.

You need a starving crowd, and the rest is truly history.
This process will be a learning curve, like riding a bike.
Once the training wheels are off, you are all set.

Kendra has played a huge role in me becoming the VP of marketing and co-owner of a multimillion-dollar network marketing company.

—Cheryl Coco, Mays Landing, New Jersey

What is the Best Strategy
for Email Marketing?

S OME BUSINESS OWNERS have a list but never email them. And if this is you, I have my arms crossed, my glasses are on, and I'm shaking my head. The hard part is over. You have your contact relationship manager set up. I'm sure you are stuck. How often should I email and what do I say? Right? The formula for daily emails used by the top 1% of online marketers is pretty simple: Something that happened to you personally and then tie that experience into how it relates to your business. I just saved you a ton of money on copywriters. No one has ever shared this one simple strategy in this way. What I just shared more than paid for the price of this book.

In marketing, emails are easily one of the most effective digital tools for driving business. It serves as a link for connecting directly to new and existing customers—a feature not found in many tools.

When potential customers find your page, whether on social media or a website, they will either engage with it or do nothing. If they aren't convinced to make a purchase, they will leave almost as quickly as they came. You probably will never see that individual on your platform again.

Emails change that dynamic. They encourage visitors to leave contact information—data that you can use to get in touch later and convert them to leads. Most of the top 1% create lead magnets to start the process of building their audience pipeline. They give valuable content to their ideal customers. This is the entire story of email-marketing strategies.

Email marketing means different things to different people. For some, it's about creating a default opt-in campaign on the landing page of their website or social media. Lead conversion won't be impressive, but a handful of customers will come through the sales pipeline. For others, it might mean sending out emails consistently to push leads further down the funnel. However, more often than not, these end up cold and produce meager results. Neither of these strategies is effective enough to bring you much success in email marketing.

There is more to email marketing than getting the contact information of potential leads. You must have a plan in place and constantly improve on it for the best strategy possible. Think of the ultimate strategy as a map that shows your position and intended destination. You just have to take the right road.

Isn't Email Marketing Dead?

People bad-mouth emails a lot, thinking it's some ancient technology that everyone has moved on from. However, the numbers beg to differ. The user base continues to expand at an astonishing rate, with projections suggesting that there will be more than 4.5 billion email users by the end of 2024.[6]

That number is proof that email is still alive and kicking and is currently one of the most effective communication channels around. Thus, email marketing is still a viable option for connecting with prospective clients and is a crucial tool to have in your marketing toolbox.

---

6   https://financesonline.com/number-of-email-users/ Accessed January 19, 2023.

However, given that more than 294 billion emails fly in several directions per day[7], it begs the question, how do you stand out and make an impression on potential customers through the haze of important, spam, and promotional emails without blowing your click-through rates?

The Ultimate Strategy

Implement functional email designs:

Your email-marketing strategy needs a solid design to be effective. Of course, an email with plain text communicates the message. But can it be better? Absolutely. An HTML email is more appealing and persuasive and will create higher click-through rates on your calls to action.

When designing your emails, create a layout of all the major elements that define your subject matter and intent, such as the footer, subject line, CTA, body text, and graphics. The top 1% use this simple formula of PAS, which means pain, agitate, and solve, in all their emails.

An email design isn't an invitation to go wild with your templates. For example, you want to prioritize readability over fanciness when choosing your fonts. Readers can

---

7   https://financesonline.com/number-of-email-users/ Accessed January 19, 2023.

then more easily absorb the information you are sharing. The simpler, the better.

You need not spend hours designing an email template from the ground up. There are lots of tools and software with libraries of customizable templates.

Clean your list:

One major challenge in email marketing that can frustrate marketers is ensuring that your campaigns make it into the inboxes of your subscribers. This phenomenon is called email deliverability.

To ensure your deliverability finds its target every time, it's imperative that you clean out your list regularly. The idea behind list cleaning is simple: get rid of every email address that has disengaged from your campaigns or unsubscribed over time.

Yes, you put a lot of time into getting that contact information and growing your list. But you can't be afraid of a little pruning. Your list gets better and brims with quality once you remove contacts that have marked your emails as spam, addresses that don't go through, unsubscribed contacts, and unengaged contacts. When you apply this, you will improve your email deliverability and brand reputation.

Subject lines matter:

About 47 percent of email recipients view mail because of the subject line alone.[8] And personalized subject lines increase the chance of being read by 50 percent.[9] These stats prove that subject lines can't be dismissed in email marketing and are crucial to the success of your campaign.

Further digging into the numbers shows that the content of your subject line isn't all that matters. The little details are just as vital, such as the number of characters involved and the sense of urgency they evoke. Subject lines between 6 to 10 words have the highest open rates,[10] while ones that sound exclusive or urgent are 22 percent more likely to be opened.[11]

Group your audience:

Understand that your audience varies according to several factors, including readiness for conversion, characteristics, and interests. As such, your content must reach the right group.

---

8   https://financesonline.com/email-subject-line-statistics. Accessed January 19, 2023.
9   Ibid.
10 Ibid.
11 Ibid.

Start by grouping clients based on uniting factors and targeting them with campaigns relevant to the grouping. For example, if customers don't want to build a relationship with the brand, invite them to sales, deals, and discounts to best encourage repeat business.

Provide value:

Your job as a marketer is about providing value. This ought to show in your email content and is pivotal to the success of your marketing strategy. If you provide value to your audience, they are more likely to look forward to and read your emails. In turn, they might invite others to join.

But how do you provide value? What does that mean?

Value is the solution to your audience's wants and needs. Providing value is meeting that need. For instance, if you are a dentist and the availability of dentures is a primary pain point for your clients, your emails should attempt to address and solve this problem.

Personalize your content:

Allow room for personalization. Let your emails find specific demographics in your audience, based on their prior purchases, interests, and other data. Curate your content to meet the needs of customers and offer them deals in line with their inclinations and preferences. Doing so creates a personalized experience, where all feel valued and welcomed.

As such, you can expect higher sales and conversion numbers, better readability, and, most importantly, the opportunity to grow, engage, and connect with your audience more effectively.

Optimize CTAs:

Why are calls to action relevant in email marketing? A marketing study on the effect of CTAs found that they are a low-cost, high-value element that brings in increased click rates.

But the type of CTA also matters. One study revealed that button-based CTAs improve click-through rates by 28 percent more than link-based CTAs.[12] Here are some tips for creating and optimizing CTAs in email marketing:

- Select and use specific copies with your target audience.

- Steer clear of words that may cause friction.

---

12 https://www.campaignmonitor.com/resources/guides/10-tips-improve-email-calls-action. Accessed January 19. 2023.

What is the Best Strategy for Email Marketing?

- Use a generous amount of white space.

- Emphasize the benefits.

- Use appropriately sized button designs that stand out.

- Analyze CTA placement.

Kendra is full of integrity and understands the marketing world from an online and offline perspective. Look no further!

—Cedrick Harris, Lutz, Florida

What Should be Included in a Referral Program?

HAVE YOU FORGOTTEN to cultivate referrals? Most businesses don't have a referral system at all. Some may have gone as far as collecting who referred to them and that's it. But for you reading this book, I want you to go a little further than that. Take the time to truly implement a referral system.

I love a certain USA automaker. When I visit my favorite salesman, he shares with me the latest and greatest in the automobile industry. In his cubicle, he has a wall covered with happy customers. His customers make it a point to share their experiences with him with their families and friends. This wall of happy customers does two things for the first-time customer. It is social proof showing not only single sales, but repeat business, as there are people on the wall more than once. He can also share stories of happy customers similar to their stories and show the photos as proof.

Referral marketing involves promoting services or products to consumers through word of mouth or referrals. It's a fairly straightforward marketing strategy that encourages others to refer their network of friends and family to your brand. While these referrals tend to occur spontaneously and independently apart from your influence, you can take charge of it and use it as an effective marketing stream.

Although word-of-mouth marketing and referral marketing seem to have similarities, they are distinct and independent of one another. The key difference is that referral marketing is a more deliberate attempt at marketing than word-of-mouth. Businesses make plans for and implement referral-marketing campaigns. They do so by encouraging their consumer base to inform others about the business.

Word-of-mouth marketing, on the other hand, is left to the consumers' discretion. If they like your brand enough, they may introduce it to their loved ones without any influence from the business.

Why Does It Work?

Here are some statistics for referral marketing:

- Referral marketing brings in five times more sales than paid advertising.[13]

- Customers who are introduced to a business via word of mouth tend to spend twice as much and introduce twice as many people to the business.[14]

- Half of Americans prefer word-of-mouth referrals as an information source for potential purchases.[15]

- Referred leads have better conversion rates (30 percent), with a 16 percent lifetime value that exceeds leads from other marketing sources.[16]

These numbers show just how powerful referral marketing can be. What's more, it's trusted and cost-effective, because when a business gives us a great experience, we tend to get others in on the action.

---

13 https://rockcontent.com/blog/referral-marketing. Accessed January 19, 2023.

14 https://writersblocklive.com/blog/word-of-mouth-marketing-statistics. Accessed January 19, 2023.

15 https://review42.com/resources/word-of-mouth-marketing-statistics. Accessed January 19, 2023.

16 https://www.linkedin.com/pulse/referred-leads-convert-30-better-have-16-higher-lifetime-ali-salman. Accessed January 19, 2023.

Winning Strategies to Gain Maximum Referrals and Boost ROI

Inform your audience:

Is it even a referral program if no one knows about it? You must enlighten your customers about the program to get them going. You want to drum up enough interest across all your platforms and marketing channels, including paid posts, email, and social media, as well as other alternative outlets. Think of your referral program as a product launch.

Ease of use:

The best referral marketing programs are easy to use. Think about how others might see it: a senior, your mom, or some random eighth grader out there. Can they figure it out and show it to their friends? How easily and quickly can they do that? If it hardly makes sense to them, you might need to rethink your strategy.

One of the most crucial areas of successful referral programs is that existing customers can easily implement them and send new customers your way to keep the cycle going. If they have to jump through many hoops to do that, the program will most likely fail.

Provide valuable incentives:

Although an overwhelming majority of customers (83 percent) say that they will refer others to a business after having a positive experience,[17] only 29 percent follow up on that.[18] You can improve your odds by giving satisfied customers a reason to introduce your business to friends and family.

Incentives can be as simple as sales discounts to more complex offers like store credits, depending on your service or product and what appeals to your consumer base the most. Ensure that your incentives are appealing enough to encourage referrals. If you don't know what incentives work in your industry, consider checking out the referral programs of competitors.

Take advantage of joint ventures and influencer marketing:

People are more likely to believe the recommendations of their friends and show relative cynicism for celebrity endorsements. But people also trust influencers, especially ones who have built credibility on reviewing products and services. It's why we see many companies

---

17 https://www.signpost.com/blog/referral-marketing-statistics. Accessed January 19, 2023.

18 https://www.forbes.com/sites/marciaturner/2016/11/30/7-effective-ways-to-boost-valuable-business-referrals. Accessed January 19, 2023.

partnering with influencers during product launches. Alternatively, businesses also align themselves with complementary businesses in a cross-promotional way. This strategy involves the referring business using incentives to encourage customers to patronize the referred business in return for a percentage of the sales.

Curate viral content:

You should primarily aim to create content that provides value. But that shouldn't stop you from aiming to go viral either. The three crucial elements for making viral content are

- identifying high-flying content in your industry or niche.

- personalizing and improving on the content and

- promoting it to your audience.

You need to know this because most businesses don't have a clue as to where to start. The best advice I received is to focus on one traffic source at a time.

When I first started many years ago, I was terrified that the process was complicated. I had heard that so many were doing well with using social media to sell their products, so I joined the party. Little did I know at the time that they were using Facebook pages and Google ads to get new customers. They had cracked the code on how to create mass audiences and turn them into customers all by using community pages.

Here's what you need to do so you can pivot to get results or start with confidence. Begin with the end in mind. Ask yourself this question: "How can I get a large group of people excited about what I offer? Is it possible to get that audience to become customers?"

And of course, the answer is yes!

The secret to how you can build an audience who will buy from you is through community-based marketing. Don't waste your hard-earned money on branding. Building an engaged community will, by default, build your brand. If you build it right, they will stay with you. Take a look at all the top 1%. They have one thing in common: They built massive audiences in a certain niche market.

Getting off the marketing roller coaster can be hard, as I mentioned before. Let's face it, Facebook is not going anywhere. You have to lean into that fact. And I will be here to help you navigate your way through the maze. Check out my easy 7-Step Traffic Accelerator Cheat Sheet (p 79).

Cash In On
Membership Clubs

NETFLIX, DISNEY+, AND Amazon Prime are great examples of membership businesses. They sell subscriptions that afford you access to the membership club and its perks. Businesses in this industry offer exclusive communities, services, products, and regular content, among other benefits.

For marketers, a membership business is a source of recurring opportunities, including building community and revenue. The best part is that you can expect repeat business because customers have to be members to get what you offer.

What You Must Know

You need to set well-defined membership packages and deals for any shot at success in membership marketing. This means you can identify your primary market and break them down, according to their needs and how you can meet said needs. For example, Netflix has several membership options based on user needs. If you only use the service on your phone, it makes sense to use the basic plan. For a family, though, the more extensive plans are better.

Besides meeting the needs of customers, you also want to implement the correct processes and systems to better support potential customers. This could mean renting a space, embedding a payment processor on your platform, or buying physical equipment for work.

Tips for Building the Perfect Membership Club

Create deals and coupons:

Everyone loves a deal. That's why people line up for hours on Black Friday or for other great sales. If that works for brick-and-mortar stores, it sure works online too. You can generate more interest in your brand and draw members to your service with coupons and deals, both online and off.

Reach out to new customers:

You could be producing the best products and services in the world, and you would still lose customers over time due to attrition rates. And that's all right because people will leave at some point. That's just proof that you need to keep working on securing new members rather than depending on existing ones. Only two things matter to the top 1% on a daily basis: how people are added to their list and their rate of KPI. Try converting leads as often as possible to keep your membership club going at all times. Use solid content-marketing strategies and Google ads to improve brand visibility and maximize outreach.

Provide value:

What does your brand do for its members? How would you answer this? More importantly, how would your customers answer it? When members know the value they stand to gain, you won't have to convince them to stay. Naturally, the high renewal and sign-up rates will be all the proof you need.

Determining and learning to express your value to prospective members is important. That's why you must take time with your pitch. Redefine the value you offer your members, both new and existing. Make sure that these benefits are present in your marketing materials and communications. Don't overlook the importance of a newsletter. For instance, create a newsletter with a personal vibe. The top 1% understand the power of getting into someone's mailbox. This way, you can better relate to your customers and keep them coming back.

Decide on potential channels and strategies:

You can use multiple channels for communication and marketing to potential members: social media, email, TV, radio, magazines, and direct mail. However, these mediums might not be enough to spread your message to a wider audience. In fact, the most popular organizations leverage more options than their counterparts. That means you have a better chance of leveraging many outreach mediums.

For instance, when creating your ideal customer profiles, investigate where prospective clients are most likely to hang out, the channels they view the most, and the type of content they consume and like. With this data, you can organically target potential new members.

Incentives:

Similar to coupons and deals, you can lure prospective clients with other incentives. This is especially useful for those who can't seem to make up their minds. Make it clear in your marketing campaigns that you are offering incentives or promotions for anyone who signs up for membership.

For instance, you can throw in some customized coffee cups, key holders, water bottles, T-shirts, pens, stationeries, etc. You also want to bring these items to special in-person events and make them available on your website.

Measure your progress:

Regularly monitoring your marketing is the best strategy for unraveling areas that need improvement and learning what produces results. You can do this by measuring performance indicators, which paint a story as to how your campaign is faring. You will see clear signs that your campaign is reaching your target market, resonating with your audience, attracting clients and generating sign ups.

It can be challenging to keep up with all the metrics. But you still need to track campaigns targeting new members. The right metric to watch, in this case, is member growth per quarter.

Set up valuable events:

In keeping with the theme of providing value, consider setting up a networking event to meet new members and catch up with existing ones. You can do this through lunch or dinner events that involve popular speakers discussing industry trends. Or you might organize a casual night to just make friends. This will keep customers referring back to the occasion and talking about you for a long time. And if it becomes a recurring affair, word-of-mouth advertisement could lure new customers. For these events, always encourage your current customers to bring their friends, colleagues, teammates, or family members.

Many online services on the internet sound helpful but fall short of delivering new customers to you. You need to be very careful because they might offer templates for your business, but not all businesses are one size fits all. Each business is unique. Business owners generally consider other factors, such as who will manage their digital marketing when they are short-staffed or putting a team in place to manage growing their audience. Their ability to create a fully customized marketing plan is limited.

So be extremely careful of wasting a lot of money on services or ideas that don't provide results. Make sure you are not going down the rabbit hole of branding your company instead of building an audience who will buy from you over and over again. The top 1% know that most entrepreneurs won't do half of what is suggested in this book. That is why they leverage these points to continuously grow their business faster.

"Kendra knows exactly how to get you out of that old-school recruiting mentality and help you propel your business online!"

—Latasha Mitchell, Maple Ridge, British Columbia

Seven-Step Traffic Accelerator

BUILDING YOUR SOCIAL media traffic or following is an art and a process that requires certain skills and specific activities. Remember that becoming a member of the top 1% means that you are not just interested in the number of customers but in building a clientele of loyal customers. To do this, you must work your way toward growing a massive social media presence.

This chapter will expose the seven secret steps that the top 1% use in accelerating their social media traffic: the Seven-Step Traffic Accelerator used by the top 1%. As of 2021, more than 79 percent of Americans use at least one social media platform.[19] According to a recent study by Pew Research Center, 70 percent of social media users log into their accounts at least once per day[20] and 49 percent multiple times in a day.[21] These figures show that a large population of people uses social media to connect, network, share information, and also seek any service. The top 1% of digital marketers leverage this huge number to acquire large a following, which makes it very easy for them to sell any product or brand. In this chapter, I will reveal the seven steps to drive massive traffic using social media.

Seven-Step Traffic Accelerator

1. Do market research: Knowing your industry is usually the very first thing the top 1% does. This also applies to social media. They first choose their desired niche based on sufficient research and studies. You must be passionate about your niche because driving traffic using organic methods will take time. Therefore, you must choose a niche that interests you, a niche for which you can easily find content or pictures or post about. On my website, I have a guide to choosing a niche for your social media page. Kindly refer

19 https://www.broadbandsearch.net/blog/social-media-facts-statistics. Accessed January 19, 2023.
20 https://www.pewresearch.org/internet/2021/04/07/social-media-use-in-2021. Accessed January 19, 2023.
21 Ibid.

to that guide so that you can select the right niche. The next thing to note while choosing your niche is its selling potential. Choose a niche that enables you to sell your products, and one that will attract potential buyers. Take care to choose a niche that properly aligns with your product so that you can easily sell them.

2. Set up your page: Depending on your choice of social media, you need to create a page, and the time to do it is now. You can call it a product page or a fan page, whatever this means to you. The goal is to have a place dedicated solely to promoting your brand with the hope of selling your product. You will first need to drive traffic to the page. The top 1% are very intentional about this step. For them, creating a page is not just using the Create New Page button of any social media but is more than that. They bring art to their page. Even without any content, this page already communicates the brand they are trying to build. So do the same or even more when creating your page. Get a graphic designer to create a professional or artistic page cover. Use a high-quality picture as your profile photo. Most importantly, everything about your page must be relevant and connected to your page title and brand. Place your phone number, website URL, email address, and your availability where they are visible so that users can easily contact you.

3. Populate your page with posts: The lifeline of any social media page is content, content, content! When creating your page, load at least thirty image posts to show that content will be frequently posted and also give early visitors something to interact with. The top 1% do not want you to know this. An image post is one where you post an image along with content. Loading thirty initial image posts lays a foundation for massive future growth. If you do not have the time to create these image posts, you can outsource this. This is also the time to create many posts and content because you will be constantly and consistently posting on your social media page.

4. Create your first page like ad campaign: Now is the time to get people to truly follow your page. Page like ads convince people to like your page. This is simply a CTA button that people will click to like and follow your page. When people like and follow your page, all new posts will appear on their social media wall. Keep in mind that this campaign does not immediately lead to product sales; rather, it is part of an overall plan for a bigger social media strategy.

5. Keep engagement high on your page: As a rule of thumb, I recommend posting eight to ten times a day. Yes, you read that right. Building high

traffic on social media requires a serious commitment from you. The top 1% are constantly doing this. Even if you need to hire someone to manage your page, never let your page go dry of content. Keep engagement up, interact in the comment section, and don't let your fans feel lonely. Engage with their comments or questions. Your daily posts should be a mixture of content, pictures, infographics, videos, or even live events (Facebook Live, Instagram Live, etc.). Make your page dynamic and interesting. Again, remember that everything you post must be related to your page title. Online tools can automate this process. I recommend the FanPage Robot, which allows you to generate viral content, the best hashtags for your post, etc. Take advantage of the great features offered by this app to grow your social media.

6. Build your list: After completing the first five steps, your page should be on its way to success, measured by evidence of consistent growth in the number of followers. Now is the time for you to get what I call your social media ROI. It is time to build your list. Building your list is the lifeblood of any internet marketer. It is your greatest asset because you are as strong as the people you can reach. This reach can be measured by the number of people you have on your list. So you will need to capture their email. To do this,

create a simple opt-in form using a free PDF or an infographic. People can then opt in by using this form. This is popularly known as a lead magnet. Once you have their email address, you can communicate directly with them via email. Take advantage of this list to send content that will loosen their wallets.

7. Monetization: After you have built your page up to at least thirty thousand followers through a page like ad campaign, now is the right time to monetize it. Do not hesitate—sell your products through this community of people. You can use different platforms to sell your products to your customers: Amazon, Shopify, AliExpress, etc. By now, you have positioned your page followers through your posts to like your products. Therefore, when you start running your product campaign, it will be easy for them to buy.

So now you have the necessary information to get new customers so you can rest easy at night.

Bonus Chapters from
Jerome Lewis

RAFFIC IS ONE of the biggest expenses we have in our business. If you are like me, you've lost a ton of money on Facebook, Google, and YouTube. I did, but I refused to quit because I knew everything I wanted was on the other side of that wall. So I continued to invest in mastering traffic acquisition skills. But then, I ran across Jerome Lewis, who was open about how to be successful with intent based marketing. He is truly one of a kind. So take notes on the secrets he's sharing here to use Google Ads as to increase traffic in your business.

Intent-Based Marketing vs Disruptive Marketing

I N THE WORLD of online marketing, businesses have two main approaches to reach their target audience: intent-based marketing and disruptive marketing. Both methods have their own unique advantages and disadvantages and understanding the difference between the two is essential for businesses seeking to achieve their marketing objectives.

Intent-based marketing is a cutting-edge approach to advertising that utilizes advanced algorithms and machine learning to understand the user's motivations, needs, and behaviors. By analyzing the user's context, preferences, and search history, intent-based marketing delivers the most relevant content, products, and services to the user, increasing the chances of a successful conversion. Key advantages of intent-based marketing include its ability to reach the right audience at the right time, its ability to deliver relevant content to users, and its ability to track results in real-time.

Disruptive marketing, on the other hand, is a traditional approach to advertising that focuses on delivering a message to a large audience and isn't as hyper-specific as intent-based marketing. This method normally focuses on a user's broad interests. This method is often used to create brand awareness and drive traffic to a website, and is typically achieved through methods such as display advertising (Meta Ads), pop-ups, and other disruptive advertising tactics. Key advantages of disruptive marketing include its ability to reach a large audience, its ability to create brand awareness, and its relatively low cost when compared to other forms of advertising.

While both intent-based marketing and disruptive marketing have their benefits, they also have limitations. Intent-based marketing can be more expensive and requires a higher level of technical expertise to implement. It can sometimes deliver irrelevant content to users, which can negatively impact the user experience.

Disruptive marketing can be less effective at driving conversions and users often consider it intrusive. Thus, disruptive marketing can have a negative impact on the user experience, as it often presents users with irrelevant and annoying advertisements.

Let's look at two examples:

Example 1

Meet Sarah, a small business owner who runs an online store selling handmade jewelry. Sarah wants to increase her sales and reach a wider audience, so she invests in online advertising. After some research, she learns about two different approaches to online advertising: intent-based marketing and disruptive marketing.

Sarah tries both approaches to see which one works best for her business. For her intent-based marketing campaign, she sets up a Google Ads account and targets users who are searching for handmade jewelry or similar products. She carefully crafts her ads to match the user's search intent and to deliver relevant content. She uses advanced targeting options to reach users who have previously visited her website or engaged with her brand on social media.

For her disruptive marketing campaign, Sarah sets up a display advertising campaign and targets users who are browsing websites related to fashion and jewelry. Her ads are eye-catching, attention-grabbing, create brand awareness, and drive traffic to her website.

After several weeks, Sarah checks her results and is surprised to see that her intent-based marketing campaign has outperformed her disruptive marketing campaign by a significant margin. Her Google Ads campaign has a higher number of clicks and conversions, and her cost per conversion is much lower than her display advertising campaign. She is also pleased to see that her ads are delivering relevant content to users, which enhances their experience driving better results.

In conclusion, intent-based marketing has proven to be the more effective option for her business, delivering better results and a better user experience. By targeting users based on their search intent, Sarah can reach the right audience at the right time, deliver relevant content, and drive better results for her business.

Example 2

Now meet John who owns a large retail company named John's Clothing, which sells a wide range of clothing and accessories for men, women, and children. John wants to increase brand awareness and drive traffic to his website, so he invests in online advertising. After doing some research, he learns about two different approaches to online advertising: intent-based marketing and disruptive marketing.

John tries both approaches to see which one works best for his business. For his intent-based marketing campaign, he sets up a Google Ads account and targets users who are searching for clothing or similar products. He carefully crafts ads to match the user's search intent and deliver relevant content. He uses advanced targeting options to reach users who have previously visited his website or engaged with his brand on social media.

For his disruptive marketing campaign, John sets up a display advertising campaign and targets users who are browsing websites related to fashion and lifestyle. His ads are eye-catching, attention-grabbing, create brand awareness, and drive traffic to his website.

After several weeks, John checks his results and is pleasantly surprised to see that his disruptive marketing campaign has outperformed his intent-based marketing campaign by a significant margin. His display advertising campaign has driven a higher number of clicks and conversions and his cost per conversion is much lower than his Google Ads campaign. He is also pleased to see that his ads have created a buzz around his brand, increasing awareness and driving more traffic to his website.

In conclusion, John's experience highlights the difference between intent-based marketing and disruptive marketing. Disruptive marketing has proven to be the more effective option for his business, delivering better results and a higher level of brand awareness. John can reach a wider audience, drive more traffic to his website, and increase brand awareness.

In conclusion, both intent-based marketing and disruptive marketing have their own unique advantages and disadvantages, and the choice between the two will depend on the specific needs and goals of the business. In the next chapter of this book, we will delve into one specific intent-based marketing platform. Google Ads has proven to be highly effective for businesses looking to maximize their reach and drive conversions. Whether a business owner or marketer pursues intent-based marketing or disruptive marketing, it is important to carefully consider the options and choose the approach that best meets the business's needs.

Google Ads and the Science of Intent-Based Marketing

I N TODAY'S BUSINESS environment, companies are under constant pressure to achieve maximum impact with their marketing efforts. To meet this challenge, many have turned to digital advertising, and one platform that has proven to be particularly effective is Google Ads. This platform leverages the science of intent-based marketing to deliver highly relevant content, products, and services to users which helps businesses maximize their reach and drive conversions.

Intent-based marketing is a data-driven approach to advertising that uses advanced algorithms and machine learning techniques to understand the user's motivations, needs, and behaviors. By analyzing the user's context, preferences, and search history, Google Ads delivers the most relevant content to the user. This increases the chances of a successful conversion and drives better results for businesses.

One of the key benefits of Google Ads is its ability to target users at the right time and place. When a user searches for a product or service, Google Ads displays the most relevant advertisements to them. This ensures it presents the user with content relevant to their needs and of value to them benefitting the business and also enhancing the user experience.

Compared to traditional disruptive marketing methods, Google Ads offers several distinct advantages. First, it allows businesses to reach a large and diverse audience, which can be difficult to achieve through traditional marketing methods. Second, Google Ads provides businesses with the ability to track their results and make real-time adjustments to their campaigns, ensuring that they are always driving the best possible results.

Besides these benefits, Google Ads also offers businesses several advanced targeting options. For example, businesses can target users based on their location, device type, search history, and more; allowing them to reach the right audience with the right message. They can also use Google Ads to reach specific audiences, such as those who have previously visited their website or engaged with their brand on social media.

In conclusion, Google Ads and intent-based marketing represent a powerful combination for businesses looking to achieve their marketing goals. By leveraging the science of intent-based marketing, businesses can reach their target audience, drive conversions, and achieve maximum impact with their marketing efforts. With its ability to deliver relevant content, track results in real-time, and provide advanced targeting options, Google Ads is a vital tool for businesses looking to succeed in today's competitive digital landscape.

And now, you're probably asking:

"So What Do I Do Next?"

At this point, I'm not asking you to hire me or to change your marketing agency.

All I am asking is that you say *maybe*.

The Most Incredible FREE Gift Ever!

$997.94 Worth of Pure
Money-Making Information

Kendra Fipps Crowe & Friends are offering an incredible opportunity for you to see why the Kendra Crowe Inner Circle is known as the place for growth where entrepreneurs seeking fast and dramatic growth and greater control, independence, and security come together. Kendra wants to give you $997.94 worth of pure money-making information, including a free month as a Diamond member of Titans 3000 Insider Circle. You will receive a free all-access pass to this private membership club where she will give you every marketing advantage to grow your business. Sign up for free. Go to: https://titans3000.com

If you're looking for the most stress-free way to get the results you desire, I've put together a very special no-cost, no-obligation, limited-time opportunity just for you.

I have set aside space in my calendar to personally meet with you and lay out a customized plan so that you can get more customers and increase your profits even in a down economy.

During our time together, you will receive

- The Ultimate Breakthrough Strategy Session: A sixty-minute live Zoom session so that you and I will have plenty of time to discuss your questions and concerns regarding getting new customers for your business in a simple, easy-to-understand form.

- A customized marketing blueprint plan so that you know exactly what steps you should take to ensure that you are not wasting your hard-earned money. You will never wonder if you are being taken advantage of.

As a bonus, you will get my free marketing tool kit. After our meeting, you will know all your options so that you can make an educated decision as to how to invest in getting new customers today, tomorrow, or ten years down the road.

I'm so confident that you'll find the **"The Ulitmate Breakthrough Strategy Session" valuable** that I'm going to give you

MY 100 PERCENT RISK-FREE GUARANTEE.

Although your consultation is free, I know your time is valuable. I also understand you might be wondering if my offer is as valuable as I say it is.

So I'm putting my money where my mouth is.

If at the end of our time together, you don't believe that it was worth your while or you feel as if I wasted your time, just let me know and not only will you get to keep your bonuses, but I will personally write a two-hundred-dollar check to the charity of your choosing.

Unfortunately, with this special offer, I can only meet with four small businesses each month, so if you delay in responding, you may be on a waiting list of up to three months. Kindly take advantage of this free offer and get on our waiting list today. Keep checking our website as two appointments will be opening in the next few weeks, and one could be yours at the link below.

www.workwithkendracrowe.com

Sincerely,
Kendra Fipps Crowe

Direct Response Marketing Specialist

7-Step Traffic Accelerator Cheat Sheet

1. Do the Market Research

2. Setup Your Page

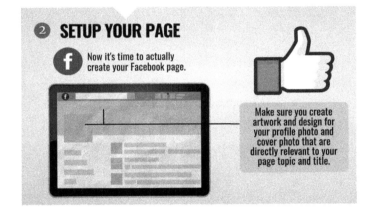

3. Populate Your Page with Posts

③ **POPULATE YOUR PAGE WITH POSTS**

30

Load at least **30 image posts** onto your page to show that content is frequently going to be posted and people have something to interact with right away when they come to your page.

8-10 TIMES A DAY

This is the laying the foundation for massive future growth! This is also the time to create a system for consistently posting content on your page 8-10 times a day.

4. Create Your First 'Like Campaing' Ad

5. Keep Engagement up on Your Page

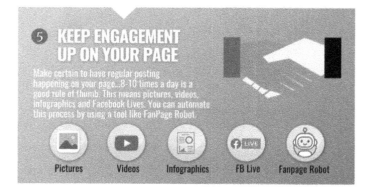

6. Time to List Build

6 TIME TO LIST BUILD!

The blood of any internet marketer is their list, after all, a list is your greatest asset of an internet marketer. You are only as strong as the people you reach. Email capturing is important and this is step six. Create a simple opt-in form and over a free infographic or PDF that people receive upon opting into your form.

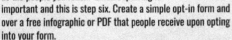

Once you have their email address you can communicate with them dierently and even begin to create oers that will loosen their wallets (step seven)!

7. Monetization is Last

MONETIZATION IS LAST

⑦

Once you've built your page up to 30,000 fans through your like campaigns AND it is thoroughly engaged, it's time to monetize! Time to sell your products through this community. You can use many different platforms to do so: Amazon, Shopify, Aliannels, .and more!

amazon | s shopify |

Want to join to the TRAFFIC SQUAD? Click Here!

What Others are Saying About Kendra

"Kendra is a rockstar when it comes to growing community pages. She's had lots of success growing pages and increasing engagement in different types of industries online. If you want to increase your online presence and engagement, I highly recommend reaching out to Kendra."

— Camilla Nymann, Odense, Denmark

"I want to talk about the marketing mindset or attitude of Kendra Fipps Crowe. First of all she is sharp, insightful and imaginative. Having an imagination along with creativity is of the utmost importance in the marketing field, and Kendra has it all. We are extremely pleased with her association with our variety of efforts with the Mound Bayou Museum and our expanding projects as we continue the quest to elevate our valuable history to the worldwide recognition it rightfully deserves. I am confident in her ability to creatively and cleverly apply her knowledge in the in all the platform areas of social media along with other forms of publicity. We look forward to our upcoming brochure and our continued rise to the top."

—Hermon Johsnon Jr., Mound Bayou, MS

Follow Kendra, follow her because she's done it. She's doing it. I'm getting advice from her. She's putting this together to give you value, that's the person I would follow closely because she's giving you a great awakening. So that's my advice for anyone, follow closer to Kendra.

—Melvin Crawley Jr, Richmond Va

Your first book is absolutely fantastic and I'm excited for your second book. For those of you out there that are, keep your eyes on Kendra. She is an upward moving rocket and it's absolutely amazing to see.

—Jim Beard, Riverview, MI

Well, you know, Kendra, I've really enjoyed working with you. I really respect you. I mean, you've come up with some incredible materials, including this summit*. It's been a pleasure to watch your journey and to see your growth and meet you in person. I expect big, big things from you and what a powerful thing you're bringing together.

— Akbar Sheikh, Dallas, TX

(*The summit is here: https://unstuckinjust15minutes.com/)

Well, I just wanna say, to anybody who's listening and watching this now, you have to understand who you're listening to. You have to understand the power that she brings to a situation, the ability to bring all of these people together to share with you is, not everybody doesn't have the ability to do that, right? Everybody doesn't have the ability to pick up the phone and call someone and say, "Hey, I wanna put something together that's gonna help thousands and thousands and thousands of people. And I think you have something to offer." She has the ability to do that. She has the ability to help you get to wherever it is you want to go. Whatever business you're in, doesn't matter. So I think that you should definitely spend a lot more time getting to know Kendra and what she does and how she does it, so that you can take full advantage of what she has to offer, what this movement, this summit* has to offer. Because, I can tell you that these relationships that you're going to develop in this situation are going to be life changing. Just make sure that you are attached to her period.

— Jason Myles, Atlanta, GA

(*The summit is here: https://unstuckinjust15minutes.com/)

I've watched, you grow over the years and I'm like, boy, Kendra is just blowing up. I mean books. I'm so proud of your accomplishments. If anybody's looking for any help in any area in business, you are that go-to person. You are just going to tell it like it is. You know, it's like, "You know that I'm concerned about your feelings in business. I'm here to make you successful in business." Cause if your, your philosophy is, you can take what I'm saying, you know, you can take the heat that I'm bringing in you, you can take the heat from anybody. And that's what, that's what I like about you because you bring it like, "Look, do it bro."

— Cedric Carr , St. Louis, MO

93

So I just really appreciate that you are putting this great awakening together for all of us to share what we have. And you are just always so generous with what you do and what you give and the resources that you provide.

Dr. Bonnie Juul, Carbdondale, IL

So really, if you're looking for a mentor who will really support you and guide you in your journey, then there's no other place to look but Kendra.

Anne Rose Rosario, Antipolo, Philippines

About the Author

KENDRA FIPPS CROWE has spent the last 15 years mastering the art of marketing, team building, coaching, and developing system to help small business owners. Helping grow their businesses by creating marketing systems has been a joy for her. She has the uncanny ability to help entrepreneurs get back on track. And this is exactly what you will find on these pages.